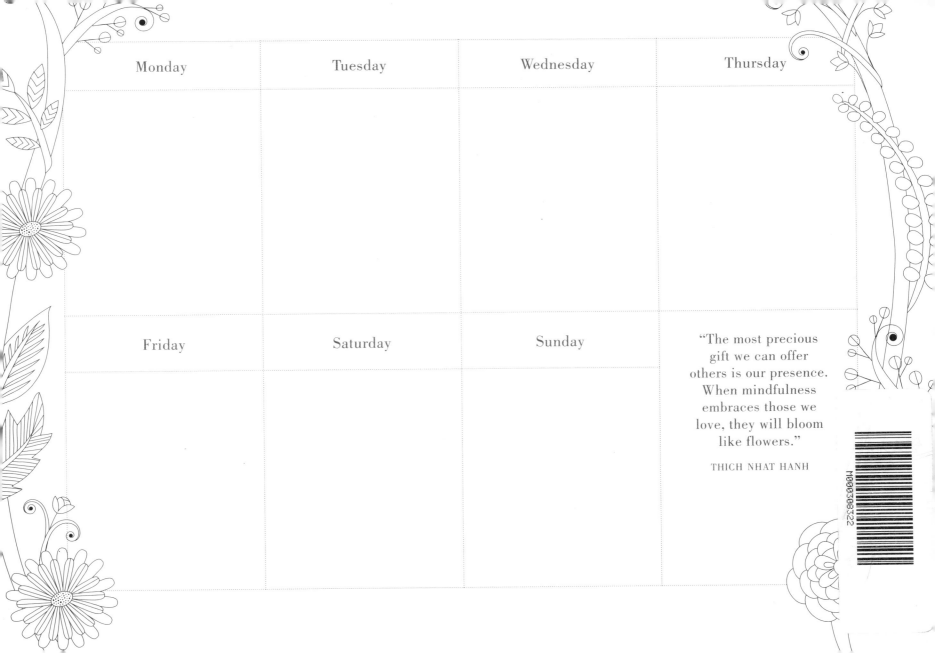

Monday	Tuesday	Wednesday	Thursday
Friday	Saturday	Sunday	

"The most precious
gift we can offer
others is our presence.
When mindfulness
embraces those we
love, they will bloom
like flowers."

THICH NHAT HANH

Monday

Tuesday

Wednesday

Thursday

Friday

Saturday

Sunday

"In this moment, there is plenty of time. In this moment, you are precisely as you should be. In this moment, there is infinite possibility."

VICTORIA MORAN

Monday

Tuesday

Wednesday

Thursday

Friday

Saturday

Sunday

"Each morning we are born
again. What we do today
is what matters most."

BUDDHA

Monday	Tuesday	Wednesday	Thursday

Friday	Saturday	Sunday	
			"The best way to capture moments is to pay attention. This is how we cultivate mindfulness. Mindfulness means being awake. It means knowing what you are doing." JON KABAT-ZINN

Monday

Tuesday

Wednesday

Thursday

Friday

Saturday

Sunday

"If you want
to conquer the
anxiety of life,
live in the moment,
live in the breath."

AMIT RAY

Monday

Tuesday

Wednesday

Thursday

Friday

Saturday

Sunday

"In today's rush, we all
think too much, seek too
much, want too much —
and forget about the joy
of just being."

ECKHART TOLLE

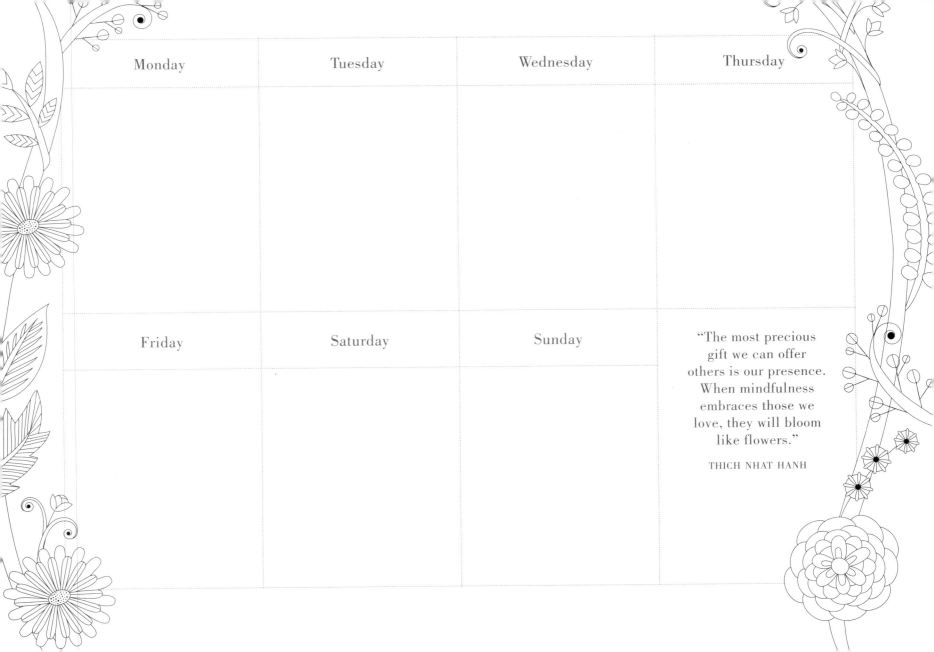

Monday

Tuesday

Wednesday

Thursday

Friday

Saturday

Sunday

"The most precious
gift we can offer
others is our presence.
When mindfulness
embraces those we
love, they will bloom
like flowers."

THICH NHAT HANH

Monday

Tuesday

Wednesday

Thursday

Friday

Saturday

Sunday

"If you want
to conquer the
anxiety of life,
live in the moment,
live in the breath."

AMIT RAY

Monday	Tuesday	Wednesday	Thursday
Friday	Saturday	Sunday	

"In today's rush, we all think too much, seek too much, want too much — and forget about the joy of just being."

ECKHART TOLLE

Monday

Tuesday

Wednesday

Thursday

Friday

Saturday

Sunday

"In this moment, there is plenty of time. In this moment, you are precisely as you should be. In this moment, there is infinite possibility."

VICTORIA MORAN

Monday

Tuesday

Wednesday

Thursday

Friday

Saturday

Sunday

"Each morning we are born
again. What we do today
is what matters most."

BUDDHA

Monday

Tuesday

Wednesday

Thursday

Friday

Saturday

Sunday

"The best way to
capture moments is
to pay attention. This
is how we cultivate
mindfulness.
Mindfulness means
being awake. It
means knowing what
you are doing."

JON KABAT-ZINN

Monday

Tuesday

Wednesday

Thursday

Friday

Saturday

Sunday

"If you want
to conquer the
anxiety of life,
live in the moment,
live in the breath."

AMIT RAY

Monday	Tuesday	Wednesday	Thursday

Friday	Saturday	Sunday	

"In today's rush, we all think too much, seek too much, want too much — and forget about the joy of just being."

ECKHART TOLLE

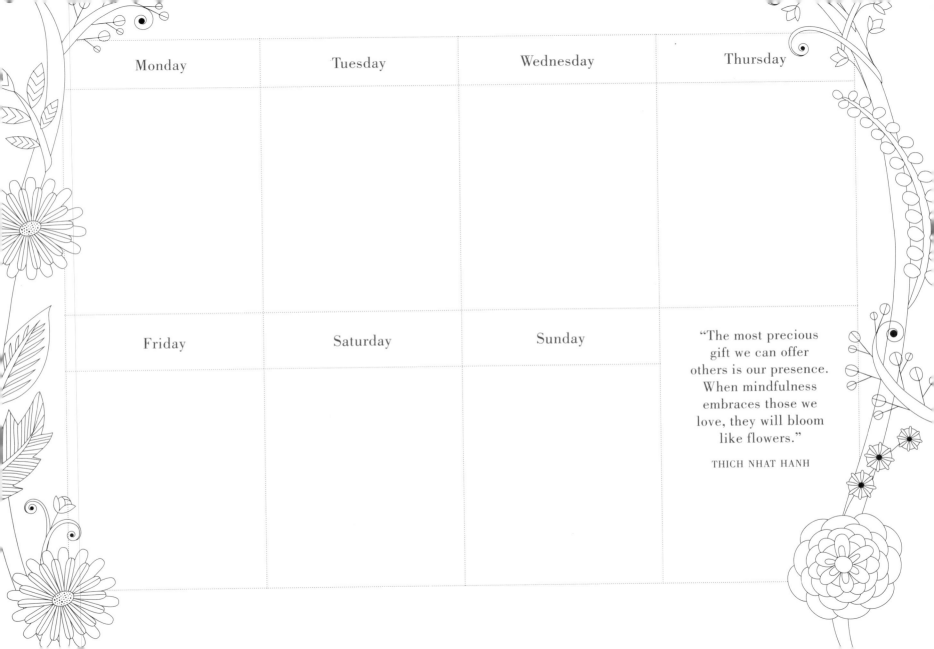

Monday	Tuesday	Wednesday	Thursday
Friday	Saturday	Sunday	"The most precious gift we can offer others is our presence. When mindfulness embraces those we love, they will bloom like flowers." THICH NHAT HANH

Monday

Tuesday

Wednesday

Thursday

Friday

Saturday

Sunday

"In this moment, there is plenty of time. In this moment, you are precisely as you should be. In this moment, there is infinite possibility."

VICTORIA MORAN

Monday	Tuesday	Wednesday	Thursday

Friday	Saturday	Sunday	"Each morning we are born again. What we do today is what matters most." BUDDHA

Monday

Tuesday

Wednesday

Thursday

Friday

Saturday

Sunday

"The best way to
capture moments is
to pay attention. This
is how we cultivate
mindfulness.
Mindfulness means
being awake. It
means knowing what
you are doing."

JON KABAT-ZINN

Monday

Tuesday

Wednesday

Thursday

Friday

Saturday

Sunday

"If you want
to conquer the
anxiety of life,
live in the moment,
live in the breath."

AMIT RAY

Monday

Tuesday

Wednesday

Thursday

Friday

Saturday

Sunday

"In today's rush, we all think too much, seek too much, want too much — and forget about the joy of just being."

ECKHART TOLLE

Monday	Tuesday	Wednesday	Thursday

Friday	Saturday	Sunday	
			"The most precious gift we can offer others is our presence. When mindfulness embraces those we love, they will bloom like flowers." THICH NHAT HANH

Monday

Tuesday

Wednesday

Thursday

Friday

Saturday

Sunday

"In this moment, there is plenty of time. In this moment, you are precisely as you should be. In this moment, there is infinite possibility."

VICTORIA MORAN

Monday

Tuesday

Wednesday

Thursday

Friday

Saturday

Sunday

"Each morning we are born
again. What we do today
is what matters most."

BUDDHA

Monday	Tuesday	Wednesday	Thursday
Friday	Saturday	Sunday	

"The best way to capture moments is to pay attention. This is how we cultivate mindfulness. Mindfulness means being awake. It means knowing what you are doing."

JON KABAT-ZINN

Monday

Tuesday

Wednesday

Thursday

Friday

Saturday

Sunday

"If you want
to conquer the
anxiety of life,
live in the moment,
live in the breath."

AMIT RAY

Monday	Tuesday	Wednesday	Thursday

Friday	Saturday	Sunday	
			"In today's rush, we all think too much, seek too much, want too much — and forget about the joy of just being."
			ECKHART TOLLE

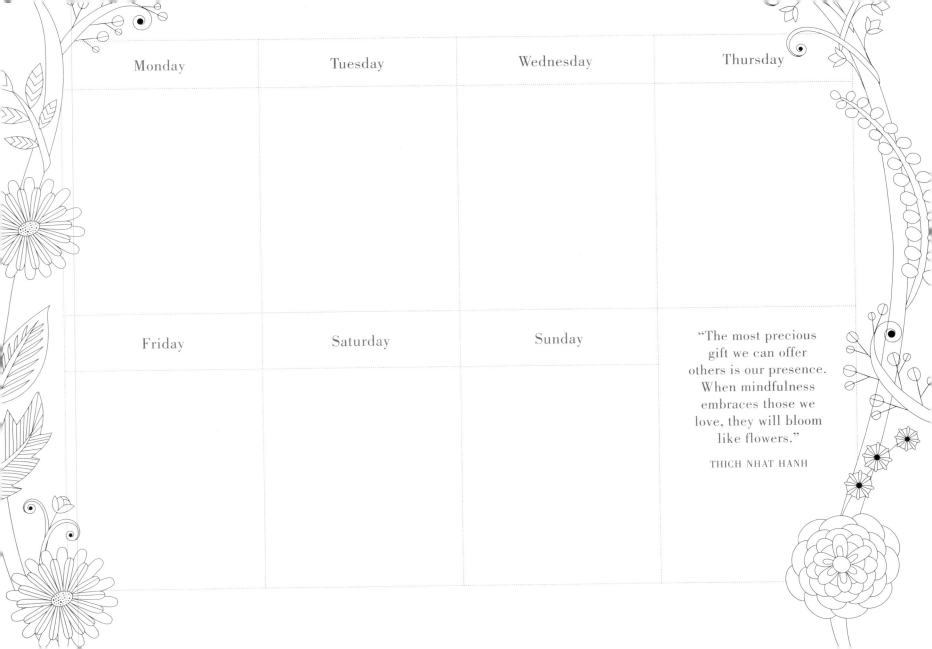

| Monday | Tuesday | Wednesday | Thursday |

| Friday | Saturday | Sunday | |

"The most precious
gift we can offer
others is our presence.
When mindfulness
embraces those we
love, they will bloom
like flowers."

THICH NHAT HANH

Monday

Tuesday

Wednesday

Thursday

Friday

Saturday

Sunday

"In this moment, there is plenty of time. In this moment, you are precisely as you should be. In this moment, there is infinite possibility."

VICTORIA MORAN

Monday

Tuesday

Wednesday

Thursday

Friday

Saturday

Sunday

"Each morning we are born
again. What we do today
is what matters most."

BUDDHA

Monday	Tuesday	Wednesday	Thursday

Friday	Saturday	Sunday	
			"The best way to capture moments is to pay attention. This is how we cultivate mindfulness. Mindfulness means being awake. It means knowing what you are doing." JON KABAT-ZINN

Monday

Tuesday

Wednesday

Thursday

Friday

Saturday

Sunday

"If you want
to conquer the
anxiety of life,
live in the moment,
live in the breath."

AMIT RAY

Monday	Tuesday	Wednesday	Thursday

Friday	Saturday	Sunday	
			"In today's rush, we all think too much, seek too much, want too much — and forget about the joy of just being." ECKHART TOLLE

Monday

Tuesday

Wednesday

Thursday

Friday

Saturday

Sunday

"The most precious
gift we can offer
others is our presence.
When mindfulness
embraces those we
love, they will bloom
like flowers."

THICH NHAT HANH

Monday

Tuesday

Wednesday

Thursday

Friday

Saturday

Sunday

"In this moment,
there is plenty of
time. In this moment,
you are precisely as
you should be. In
this moment, there is
infinite possibility."

VICTORIA MORAN

Monday

Tuesday

Wednesday

Thursday

Friday

Saturday

Sunday

"Each morning we are born
again. What we do today
is what matters most."

BUDDHA

Monday

Tuesday

Wednesday

Thursday

Friday

Saturday

Sunday

"The best way to
capture moments is
to pay attention. This
is how we cultivate
mindfulness.
Mindfulness means
being awake. It
means knowing what
you are doing."

JON KABAT-ZINN

Monday

Tuesday

Wednesday

Thursday

Friday

Saturday

Sunday

"If you want
to conquer the
anxiety of life,
live in the moment,
live in the breath."

AMIT RAY

Monday	Tuesday	Wednesday	Thursday

Friday	Saturday	Sunday	

"In today's rush, we all
think too much, seek too
much, want too much —
and forget about the joy
of just being."

ECKHART TOLLE

Monday	Tuesday	Wednesday	Thursday
Friday	Saturday	Sunday	

"The most precious gift we can offer others is our presence. When mindfulness embraces those we love, they will bloom like flowers."

THICH NHAT HANH

Monday

Tuesday

Wednesday

Thursday

Friday

Saturday

Sunday

"In this moment,
there is plenty of
time. In this moment,
you are precisely as
you should be. In
this moment, there is
infinite possibility."

VICTORIA MORAN

Monday

Tuesday

Wednesday

Thursday

Friday

Saturday

Sunday

"Each morning we are born
again. What we do today
is what matters most."

BUDDHA

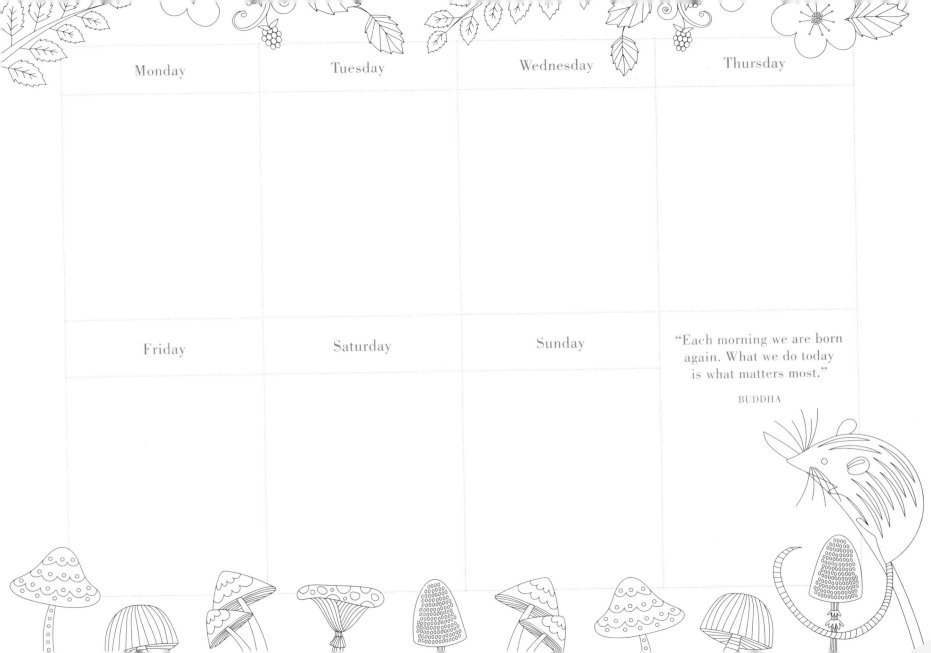

Monday	Tuesday	Wednesday	Thursday

Friday	Saturday	Sunday	
			"The best way to capture moments is to pay attention. This is how we cultivate mindfulness. Mindfulness means being awake. It means knowing what you are doing." JON KABAT-ZINN

Monday

Tuesday

Wednesday

Thursday

Friday

Saturday

Sunday

"If you want
to conquer the
anxiety of life,
live in the moment,
live in the breath."

AMIT RAY

Monday	Tuesday	Wednesday	Thursday

Friday	Saturday	Sunday	"In today's rush, we all think too much, seek too much, want too much — and forget about the joy of just being." ECKHART TOLLE